Ivan a

Hattie Naylor

Methuen Drama

Published by Methuen Drama 2010

Methuen Drama, an imprint of Bloomsbury Publishing Plc.

3 5 7 9 10 8 6 4 2

Methuen Drama
Bloomsbury Publishing Plc
50 Bedford Square
London WC1B 3DP
www.methuendrama.com

ISBN 978 1 408 14041 3

A CIP catalogue record for this book is available from
the British Library

Typeset by MPS, a Macmillan Company

Ivan and the Dogs

by Hattie Naylor

First developed by Pier Productions Limited for BBC Radio.

The ATC/Soho Theatre co-production was developed with support from
The North Wall Arts Centre.

The first performance of *Ivan and the Dogs* took place at the Drum Theatre
Plymouth on 29 September 2010. It opened at Soho Theatre on
12 October 2010.

An ATC/Soho Theatre co-production

Ivan and the Dogs

by Hattie Naylor

Cast and Creative Team

Ivan	Rad Kaim
Director	Ellen McDougall
Designer	Naomi Wilkinson
Lighting Designer	Katharine Williams
Composer and Sound Designer	Dan Jones
Movement Director	Joanna Croll
Dramaturg	Nina Steiger
Casting Director	Nadine Rennie CDG
Video Artist	Simon Dinsett
Voice Coach	Sarah Stephenson
Production Manager	Nick Ferguson
Company Stage Manager	Martha Mamo
Technical Stage Manager/Relighter	Rowan Pashley
Audio Visual Consultant	Paul Swarbrick
Set construction	Steel the Scene
Unseen characters	Max Bollinger, Oleg Dzhabrailov, Marusiya Kalinina, Oleg Kalninsh, Anastasia Mara, Basher Savage, Andrei Zayats
Children's voices	Pupils from Russian School Druzhba and Russian Association Sputnik

With thanks to:
Carl Miller and Tony Graham from the Unicorn Theatre. Emily Gray from Trestle Theatre. Jeremy Howe and BBC Radio 4. Peter Hoare, Dave Thomas, Jane Ellison and all at Pier Productions. Ben Tavener and Masha Slonim. Nadia Taylor and Toby Rushton. Lee Lyford, Tom Wainwright and Tom Glenister. Sharon Clark, Kate Yedigaroff and all at Bristol Old Vic. And with special thanks to Mr Paul Dodgson.

Lucy Maycock, Nick Quartley and all at The North Wall Arts Centre, Caroline, Will Tuck, Karla, Rosamund Bartlett, Oxana Gouli, Charlotte Hobson, Davina Kateb, Justin Salinger, Evgeny Shirkin, Bijan Sheibani and Dr Emma Widdis.

Collaborators who have supported the development process:
Sam Booth, Sam James, Rhys Rusbatch, Jonah Russell, Sophie Scott and Rebecca Whitehead.

Hattie Naylor (Playwright)

Hattie was studying painting at the Slade School of Art when her first play was accepted in the BBC Radio Young Playwrights Festival. She then went on to study mime, and set up and ran the art club Puzzle Club with David Ellis, before concentrating on writing.

She has won several national and international awards for her plays and has had a number of her short stories broadcast on Radio 4, including *Mathilde*, which opened the Bath Literary Festival in 2008. Recent broadcasts for BBC Radio include *Solaris, The Making of Ivan the Terrible*, based around an archived conversation between Eisenstein and Stalin, *Ivan and the Dogs*, and her adaptation of Samuel Richardson's *Clarissa* for the Classic Serial.

Theatre and opera work include *Mother Savage* for Travelling Light, the opera *Odysseus Unwound* for Julian Grant and Tête à Tête, and *The Nutcracker* for Theatre Royal Bath. Current projects include *Ben Hur* for the Theatre Royal Bath, *Alice Through the Looking Glass* for The Egg, Theatre Royal Bath, *Samuel Pepys' Diaries* for BBC Radio 4, and an opera with Will Gregory (Goldfrapp), conducted by Charles Hazlewood, for the Southbank in March 2011.

Rad Kaim (Ivan)

Theatre credits include *The Tempest* (Manchester Royal Exchange Theatre), *Guernica* (Oval House), *Serenade* (East River Comedia, New York), *Victory, Romeo and Juliet* (Contemporary National Theatre, Poland). Film credits include *The Empty Plan* (Kirshner & Panos), *Some Dogs Bite* (Kindle Entertainment), *Patagonia* (ITV WALES), *Harry Brown* (Marv Films), *Eastern Promises* (Kudos Pictures Ltd), *It's a Free World* (Sixteen Films). Television credits include *Waterloo Road* (BBC), *Na Dobre I Na Zle* (TVP), *Taggart* (SMG productions), *Waking the Dead* (BBC), *Dalziel and Pascoe* (BBC), *Blue Murder* (ITV), *The Bill* (ITV), *Doctor Who* (DW Productions for BBC). Rad was voted Poland's Best Newcomer in 2004 in Poland's equivalent to the Oscars.

Ellen McDougall (Director)

Ellen is Artistic Associate at ATC, and an Associate Reader at Soho Theatre.

Ellen's directing credits include *The Invisible Woman* by Rebecca Lenkiewicz (work-in-progress, ATC/Young Vic), two short new plays in *Tri-Umph*, (Oxford Playhouse), *London Lite* (reading, Soho Theatre), *Betting On The Dust Commander* by Suzan-Lori Parks (Albany Theatre Studio, UK Premiere) *Philadelphia Here I Come!* by Brian Friel and *Cymbeline* (Bedlam Theatre). Ellen was Director in Residence at the NT Studio 2009, and has directed various readings and workshops there including a devised piece about St. Kilda that was scratched at The Arches in 2010. Ellen was Staff Director at the National Theatre 2009-2010, assisting on *Women Beware Women* (dir. Marianne Elliott), *The Cat in the Hat* (dir. Katie Mitchell), and *Our Class* (dir. Bijan Sheibani). She was Assistant Director on *Tunnel 228* (Punchdrunk), and *The Brothers Size* (dir. Bijan Sheibani) and has led workshops for the Young Vic, ATC and the National Theatre. She completed the Directors Lab at the Lincoln Center in 2010, and the National Theatre Studio Directors Course in 2008. Ellen was awarded the Runner-Up Prize, funded by the Ian Ritchie Foundation, in the James Menzies-Kitchin Award 2008, and directed a workshop on *A Kind of Alaska* by Harold Pinter at BAC.

Naomi Wilkinson (Designer)

Naomi trained at the Motley Theatre Design Course after a B.A (hons) in Fine Art at Bristol.

Recent productions include: *Alice* (The Crucible Theatre, Sheffield), *Christ Deliver Us* (Abbey Theatre, Dublin), *The Fahrenheit Twins* (Barbican Pit Bite 09, Told By An Idiot/Drum Theatre Plymouth/Unity Theatre), *The Last Witch* (Edinburgh International Festival), *Peer Gynt* (Barbican Bite 09, National Theatre of Scotland/Dundee Rep, which won her the Scottish Critics' Award for Best Design 2008), *La Dispute* (Abbey Theatre, Dublin), *Cockroach, The Dogstone, Nasty, Brutish and Short* and *Nobody Will Ever Forgive Us* (Traverse Theatre/ National Theatre of Scotland).

Other recent credits include *Critical Mass* (Almeida Opera), *A Midsummer Night's Dream* (Dundee Rep, which won her the Scottish Critics' Award for Best Design 2007), *On Religion*, and *Colder than here*, both at Soho Theatre, *Happy yet?* (Gate Theatre), The site-specific project *Don't Look Back* for Dreamthinkspeak seen at the Brighton and Edinburgh festival and Somerset House London, *Casanova (West Yorkshire Playhouse), The Firework-Maker's Daughter (Lyric Theatre Hammersmith), I'm a Fool to Want You (Battersea Arts Centre), A Little Fantasy (Soho Theatre), Shoot Me in the Heart (Gate Theatre), I Can't Wake Up (Lyric Studio), Happy Birthday Mr Deka D (Traverse Theatre)*, and the award winning *I Weep at My Piano (Battersea Arts Centre)* all for Told by an Idiot with whom she has worked regularly.

Her designs for dance include: *Just for Show* for DV8 at the National Theatre, *Glacier* (Tilted Dance, QEH, South Bank), *NQR Scottish* Dance Theatre (UK Tour).

Katharine Williams (Lighting Designer)

Katharine Williams is a lighting designer working in drama, dance and physical theatre, with some opera, musical and circus projects. Katharine works in the UK and internationally. Her designs have been seen in China, Hong Kong, New Zealand, Canada, the USA, Mexico, Ireland, Holland, Spain, Italy, Germany, Armenia, Romania, Russia and the Czech Republic. She has collaborated with some of the UK's most exciting emerging artists and companies, as well as with established companies including Aldeburgh Music, the National Theatre of Scotland and the Royal Opera House in London.

Recent projects include *The Goat* at Traverse Theatre, Edinburgh and *Reykjavik* at the Edinburgh Festival Fringe, as well as Katharine's first experience of working on film, on *The Half-Light*. Forthcoming projects include *The Butterfly Effect* in Hong Kong and *Faeries* at The Royal Opera House, London.

Katharine works as a guest lecturer in lighting design for the Royal Welsh College of Music and Drama and is a co-director of Daedalus.

Dan Jones (Composer and Sound Designer)

Theatre Sound Design and Music includes *Through a Glass Darkly* (Almeida), *Kursk* (Young Vic / Sound&Fury), *England* (NT / Whitechapel Gallery), *War Music, The Watery Part of the World, Ether Frolics, Going Dark* (Sound&Fury), *A Prayer for My Daughter* (Young Vic), *Fall* (RSC / Traverse), *Slippage* (Rambert Dance Company), *Othello, The Turn of the Screw, Uncle Vanya* (Bristol Old Vic), *Each Day Dies with Sleep* (Orange Tree), *Betrayal* (Northcott), *Happy Days, A Midsummer Night's Dream* (Dundee Rep), *Coriolanus, The Changeling, The Taming of the Shrew, Julius Caesar, The Tempest* (Shakespeare at the Tobacco Factory), *So Long Life* (Bath Theatre Royal), *Spike* (Nuffield Theatre).

Feature Film Music includes *Max* (Ivor Novello Award Best Film Score), *Shadow of the Vampire, Manolete, Tomorrow La Scala* (BAFTA nominated, Cannes Selection), *The Tonto Woman* (Oscar nominated for best short film), *Four Last Songs, Twockers, Set it Loose.*

Television Music includes *Criminal Justice* (2009), *Dead Set, David Attenborough's Darwin and the Tree of Life, Murder by Numbers, Sahara, Visions of Heaven and Hell, True Stories: The Death Train, One Night Stand, Boogie Nights in Suburbia, Strange, Modern Times, The Ghosts of Rwanda, The Life of Mammals, Longitude, The Spectre of Hope, A Company of Soldiers.*

Art Installations include *Suburban Counterpoint: Music for Seven Ice Cream Vans (LIFT, NNF10), Sky Orchestra* (Fierce Festival, RSC, Sydney Festival), *Dream Director* (ICA, Arnolfini and tour) *Listening Posts* (Cork Harbour), *Tunnel Vision*. He has also produced string Arrangements for Alpha and Jarvis Cocker.

He recently co-directed Kursk at the Young Vic for Sound&Fury for whom he is joint artistic director.

Joanna Croll (Movement Director)

Joanna trained as a Movement Director under Trish Arnold and Shona Morris. She has worked extensively as a Movement Tutor at Rose Bruford College, The Drama Centre, Goldsmiths University, Florida State University, Marymount College and for The Factory and The Workshop (established by Di Trevis at The Jerwood Space). As a Movement Director/Choreographer credits include: *The Lion and The Unicorn* (Eastern Angles), *A Midsummer Night's Dream, The Tempest* and *As You Like It* (Sprite Productions), *Twelfth Night* (Pendley Shakespeare Festival) and *Someone Who'll Watch Over Me* (Diorama Arts) She is also a scholarship student of The Historical Dance Research Committee based at the Royal Academy of Dancing.

As an Actress, theatre includes: *Oh What a Lovely War* (Northern Stage), *Hamlet* and *The Seagull* (The Factory), *Private Lives* (Iceni), *The Haunted Hotel* (The Belgrade), *Anne of Green Gables* (Sadlers Wells), *Marieluise* and *Habitats* (The Gate), *Twelfth Night, Romeo and Juliet* and *A Midsummer Night's Dream* (Sprite Productions), *Wicked Women* (Arcola), *Young Woodley* and *Tea and Sympathy* (The Finborough), *The 39 Steps* (European Arts Company, Athens), *Medea* (Sheffield Crucible), *When we are Married, Stepping Out* and *Pack of Lies* (Southwold/Aldeburgh) and *The Bitter*

Tears of Petra von Kant (Flaming Theatre). Television includes: *Best: His Mother's Son* (BBC), *Sensitive Skin* (BBC), *The Girl in the Café* (BBC), *Doctors* (BBC), *The Commander VII* (ITV), *Dirty War* (BBC) and *Fallen* (ITV). Film: *Hereafter, Venus, Lady Godiva, Fakers* and *A Picture of Me.*

Nina Steiger (Dramaturg)
Nina is Associate Director at Soho Theatre and leads the Writers' Centre there. Prior to this post, Nina worked for seven years in the New York and regional theatres with such organisations as Ensemble Studio Theatre, New York Stage & Film and Hartford Stage Company alongside freelance work with companies such as The Foundry Theatre, Roundabout Theatre and Manhattan Theatre Club.

Nina also serves as a freelance dramaturg for screen writers, is on the editorial boards of Brand literary journal and Theatre Forum magazine and is a Board member for ON Theatre and proto-type theater, an International Affiliate Member of the League of Professional Theatre Women and a consultant for the UK Style Council and INN, an international performance project. As a writer, her work has been commissioned, produced and published in London, New York and Montreal.

Nadine Rennie CDG (Casting Director)
Nadine is Casting Director at Soho Theatre where credits include *Behud, Shraddha, Dreams of Violence, Roaring Trade, Iya-Ile (The First Wife), Joe Guy, Pure Gold, Piranha Heights, Baghdad Wedding, The Estate* and *An Oak Tree.* Freelance work includes *Orphans* (Paines Plough), *What Fatima Did...* (Hampstead Theatre), *Beau Jest* (Hackney Empire), *The Butterfly Club* (Southwark Playhouse), *Jesus Hopped The 'A' Train, The Long Road* and *Write Now II* (all Synergy Theatre Project), *Pressure Drop, On Religion* and *On Emotion* (all On Theatre). Nadine is a member of the Casting Directors Guild.

Martha Mamo (Company Stage Manager)
Martha studied stage management at the Royal Welsh College of Music and Drama. Theatre credits include: *Light Shining On Buckinghamshire, Pieces of Vincent* (Arcola Theatre), *Breathing Irregular, Kreutzer Sonata* (Gate Theatre), *Kursk* (Sound & Fury, Fuel), *Duet For One* (Lee Dean), *A Miracle, The Pride* (Royal Court Theatre), *Chess in Concert* (Heartache Production), *Parade* (Donmar Warehouse), *One Flew Over The Cuckoo's Nest* (Nimax), *The Changeling* (Cheek By Jowl), *Aladdin* (Old Vic Theatre), *The Bull, Flowerbed* (Fabulous Beast), *Julius Caesar* (BITE), *Pam Ann Wants You, How to Lose Friends And Alienate People* (Soho Theatre).

Rowan Pashley (Technical Stage Manager/Relighter)
Rowan began his career at the Junction in Cambridge, before moving on to the Cambridge Arts Theatre. Since becoming freelance, Rowan has toured theatre and dance extensively both nationally and internationally. Rowan is one of the partners in illuminatedesign, a production management and events services company based in Cambridge.

Paul Swarbrick (Audio Visual Consultant)
Paul trained at De Montfort University in lighting, sound and AV design and since then has worked on a variety of projects including; *A Real Human Person Who Cares And All That* (Arcola); *How the Koala Learnt to Hug* (PTC Tour); *Reykjavik* (Shams) and *Miracle on 34th Street* (Farnham Maltings) as well as numerous music acts ranging from Jools Holland to The Reading Symphonic Orchestra.

Ivan and the Dogs

Cast

Ivan

Author's note: The dialogue in Soundscapes is spoken in Russian.

Ivan So. All the money went and there was nothing to
buy food with.

Mothers and fathers couldn't feed their children
or their animals.

Mothers and fathers tried all sorts of things to
find money to buy food, but there wasn't any
because all the money was gone.

So mothers and fathers tried to find things they
could get rid of, things that ate, things that drank
or things that needed to be kept warm. They
looked about their apartments for these
things.

The dogs went first.

They took them in their cars and drove them to
the other side of the city and left them there.

But still there was no money.
So mothers and fathers looked for other things,
other things that ate, and drank and needed to be
kept warm.

And some
children

were taken to the other side of the city

and left.

Then I was four.

Four.

So I can't remember everything because I was very little but I will tell you as much as I can.

I will tell you as if it's now.

And this is now.

* * *

Soundscape. Door slamming shut. Stumbling. Man muttering in Russian. Rummaging in kitchen through cupboards – sound of bottles. Man and woman arguing.
  – Where is it? Where is it?
  – Kolya?
  – You've had all the vodka, you fucking bitch.
  – No.
  – You have. Look at you. (To **Ivan**.*) What you looking at?*
  – Leave him alone.

This is my mother and my stepfather.

Soundscape.
  – Did you drink it?
Ivan *– No.*
  – Don't hit him.

*– Shut up, bitch. (scream) Why is he here? All he does is eat and
    drink.*
– No, Kolya. No, Kolya.
– Out of my way.
*(Thud. Screaming. Mother and father fight. **Ivan** screams.)*

Every night is like this.

*Soundscape. Thud. Screaming. Mother and father fight. **Ivan**
screams.*
– No, Kolya. No, Kolya.
– Out of my way.
– No.
(Thud. Screaming. Mother and father fight. Mother screams.)
– No.
(Violent banging escalating, Mother's terrified screams.)

In the morning he will beg her to forgive him and

promise on his mother's life that he will never

hit her again. And she will say it is because we

have nothing.

She will say it is because he has not been paid for

months and months, that it is because

the bosses steal – and then she will blame the

boss of everybody who is called President Yeltsin.

And then she will cry and he will cry,

and she will tell him that he has a soft heart,

and then she will kiss his red face all over.

And he will promise again on his mother's life

that he will never hit her again.

But he is lying.

His mother should have died many times.

Soundscape.
  – *No, Kolya. No.*
  – *What's the fucking point of him? It's either me or that little shit. All he does is eat and drink. Get fucking rid of him. Get rid of him now. You hear me, bitch? It's either him or me.*
  – *No, Kolya. Don't hit him. No. NO.*
(*Child screaming.*)

And he says all I do is eat and drink. He says she

has to get rid of me. He says I have to go

and then he hits her again for keeping me.

And his breath smells like there's a dragon inside

him and tonight he builds red mountains across my

skin and the mountains are like holes

inside me. He digs into me saying forever and

forever and forever, this will be forever and

forever and forever. It will always be like this.

And he throws my mother against the walls

and she is bleeding and can't cry any more.

And I can't scream any more.

I can't even say stop.

And it is May and the ice on the river has just

broken.

And outside there are other children.

So,

I put in my pockets two packets of crisps, some dry
bread and some pickles.

I put on my thick coat and my thick gloves.

But first I go into my room and take a picture I have
of her, of my mother.
I fold it carefully so there are no lines across her
face and put it in my pocket.
And when I come back into the kitchen
they are curled around each other on the floor,
holding hands.
They sleep.
I hear them talking in their sleep.

Soundscape. Sleepy mutterings.
(*Door opening and shutting.*)

I go.
The lift is broken.
People say they will come to
mend it but they never do.
So I go down the stairs.

The door at the bottom is really thick –
and I can't open it.
It's so no one can get in.

When people get in that don't live here, there's always screaming. Two people died in the apartment next door. There were guns and then silence.

It's when God is counting.

'One, two.

Two of you go to heaven now.

Shh.

Go to heaven now, shhh, go to heaven now.'

Sshh.

I wait.

Soundscape. Big metal door opening. Laughter. Sound of pressing button for lift. Man and woman.
  – The lift doesn't work.
  – Which floor do you live on?
  – Sixteenth. Sorry.
  – Come on – up the stairs. (Giggling.)

It is Nina, she lives above us, and a man I don't know.

I run past them.

Soundscape. Man and woman.
  – Ow. Ivan, is that you? Ivan. (Shouting after him.) Ivan!
  – Let him go.
  – Ivan!

– He's gone now. Come on. We've got things to do.
(Giggling. They move off.)

I'm out. It is night time.

Into the wild, wild world.

* * *

And this is the first night.

It is cold and wet.

The streets are empty.

I can't find anywhere to sleep.

Everything is wet and smells.

I see someone lying on some cardboard in the doorway of a shop.

So I do the same. This must be how you sleep here.

I lie on the cardboard and put cardboard on top of me.

I sleep.

But I am woken by a boy kicking me.

Soundscape. Boy.
 – *You can't stay here.*

He tells me that I can't stay here.

Soundscape. Boy *shouting.*
 – *Pay! Pay!*

You have to pay to stay here, he says.

Soundscape. Boy *shouting.*
 – *Pay! Pay!*

So I run. And I hear him laughing at me.

Telling me I am stupid.

Soundscape. Laughter.
Boy.
– *Stupid kid. Just left home, have you? You're not going to get far like that.*

I have to find some children who will like me.

A babushka opens a kiosk, slowly, as if she is

not really awake.

Then she sits inside, smoking and talking to herself.

I am standing in front of her, but she does not

see me.

I walk towards the kiosk.

She stands up and shouts at me.

Soundscape. Woman.
– *Get away. Go away.*

I go back to where I was and she stops shouting,

sits down and talks to herself again.

I don't think she can see me any more.

And someone has emptied a bin on to the street.

And rubbish blows everywhere.

And everything smells.

I take out one of my packets of crisps and

eat them.

I walk about the city.

No one notices me.

And when it is night, I hide

so no one will kick me.

I hide in the streets away from the ones with shops.

There are packs of dogs there too.

They frighten me.

They are big dogs.

They hunt together.

I eat my last packet of crisps and dried bread.

And in the morning I find some sweets in a bin.

* * *

I go to a place there is only rubbish.

I watch two children disappear into the ground.

Then two other children come up.

Then another three come up.

Maybe these children will be my friends.

Soundscape. Children giggling.

They smile.

I don't think they can feel the cold.

There's a hole in the ground.

I stand over the hole and look in.

Maybe somewhere in the earth there's a kind

mother that makes you happy.

I go in.

Inside it's dark with pipes that go on forever.

There are candles and it stinks.

The pipes are warm and children lie on them.

The children are very still

and blow plastic bags up in their mouths,

like balloons.

Then a boy stands in front of me.

Soundscape. **Boy.**
   – *Glue. You want some glue?*

    'Glue,' he says. 'You want some glue?'

    I don't know what he means.

Soundscape. **Boy.**
   – *Glue. Glue.*

    I say, 'Yes.'

Soundscape. **Boy.**
   – *What can you give me?*
   – *You can't have any glue unless you pay me, you idiot.*

    He says I can't have any glue if I can't pay.

    And he pushes me to the floor.

    Then I look at the children next to me,

    blowing the plastic bags in their mouths.

    Their eyes aren't good.

    'Nothing is wrong with the world,' one says.

    Then he shouts it.

    'Nothing, nothing now, is wrong with the world.'

Soundscape. **Boy.**
   – *Nothing is wrong with the world!*
(*Children laughing.*)

    Then the bully boy searches my pockets.

He takes out my packet of sweets and eats them.

Then he takes my picture of my mother.

Soundscape. Boy.
   – This isn't enough to buy glue.

He tells me this isn't enough to buy glue.

All I want is my picture back.

I say,

'I don't want to buy any glue anyway.

I don't want to look like there's nothing in my

eyes.'

Soundscape. Boy.
   – Why? Do you have so much to live for?
(Children laughing.)

And he says why? Is it because I have so much to

live for?

And he kicks me and

screws up my picture of my mother and throws

it in my face.

'Get out,' he shouts. 'You have to pay to live here.

Soundscape. Boy.
   – Get out!!

And he comes near to kick me

again. And all the children are shouting,

'Kick him, kick him hard.'

Soundscape. Children.
   – *Kick him. Kick him. Kick him!! (etc.)*
(*Children laughing.*)

        I pick up my picture

        and run, and some of the other children

        try and trip me up as I run through them,

        and I fall and they laugh.

        And then I am climbing back up

        into the cold.

        And I run till I stop.

        Then I take the picture of my mother

        And smooth it out against the ground.

        She has lines all over her face

        from where the bully boy screwed it up.

        A dog is watching me.

        Her eyes are hungry.

        I am afraid of her.

        She is big and she could hurt me.

        She is still.

        She sniffs the air. I have no food.

        Then she turns and goes away.

        Maybe she is afraid too.

I got water from the melting snow. But you have to
have lots and lots of it to stop feeling thirsty.

It is very cold.

* * *

Soundscape. Humming Bombzi.
Bonfire.

There's a fire.

Drunk men round it.

Bombzi – drunk street men that no one wants.

They are roasting potatoes.

One stands away from the others.

He is looking at a lump in the snow.

Soundscape. (Like howls, away off.)
  – Vlad!
  – Vlad! Vlad!

And he starts to cry.

Soundscape. Men and women. (Man crying.)
  – Vlad!
  – Vlad! Vlad!
  – Vlad, our friend.
  – He was a good, good man.

It is a body.

The winter killed him.

The winter kills lots of Bombzi.

You see the bodies when May comes and
everything melts.

They stand round the body crying for him.

One of the crying ones sees me. I go to run but then
he holds out a potato for me.

I take it and stand away.

Soundscape. Singing or humming, mumbling between.
Man.
  – *Dear boy, dear boy.*

He sings and moves closer to me.

Soundscape. Singing or humming, mumbling between.
Man.
  – *Dear boy, dear sweet boy.*

He puts his large hand on my shoulder.

And I see the dog again.

She is white.

She watches me.

Soundscape. Singing or humming, mumbling between.
Man.
  – *My dear boy, my dear boy.*

But I see there is no good in him
even with tears in his eyes.

He wants something bad from me.

The white dog is hungry too and she barks.

I think she sees it too, the bad thing in him.

He moves closer again, he is standing over me.

I can smell his dragon's breath.

And I don't know what to do.

She barks again.

I push him hard.

And I run with my potato.

Soundscape.
Man.
  – *Come back! Come back, you little git. Come back! Come back!*

The white dog runs.

We are running together.

And we stop.

A long way away from the Bombzi.

We both breathe very hard.

We are by a big factory.

I sit.

She sits.

I break off a bit of my potato and put it in my hand.

I lay my hand open for her to take it.

(*Referring to hand.*) Potato in my hand.

I wait.

We wait together.

But she won't take it.

She just looks down on the ground with big hungry

sad eyes and I am not frightened of her any more.

I think very sad eyes.

So I put the potato on the ground.

I move away.

Now she comes near to the potato, very near.

And then snaps it up.

Now she eats it.

I stand as far away as I was from the Bombzi

so I cannot hurt her.

I would never hurt her.

I eat the rest of my potato – giving her two more bits.

She waits for me.

She sighs. I sigh.

I close my eyes.

Then I sleep. I sleep knowing she is watching me –

knowing the white dog watches me.

* * *

In the morning the white dog has gone.
I take the picture of my mother out of my
pocket but I still can't make the lines go.
One day my mother will be kind and
beautiful again and she will be happy when
I come home.
And we will live on our own in a place with a
garden. And when I go home I will bring
her lots of packets of crisps.
Bacon flavour. (*stop*)

I am at the back of the factory.
It is a large building made of metal.
and everything smells burnt and dirty.
And nothing is tidy.

And now the men are coming to work.
So I hide.

Then I see her again. The white dog.
She knows I'm there. Though the men don't.
She is careful not to get near them and then
I see her disappear underneath the building.
This is her den.
There are other dogs that live in her den.

And now I am so hungry.

I hide near the factory door.

It is very noisy and I watch the men.

Their eyes are covered.

They are making sparks.

All morning this hungry feeling grows.

But I think that the day is not very safe if

you are small.

The dogs know this.

They stay in their den, so I stay in my hiding place.

The men come out for lunch.

When the men come out they are black all over.

And their eyes are the only thing

that is a colour.

Then they throw what they don't want away

and they go back in.

The white dog moves towards the bin when they

have gone back but she can't get inside.

When she sees me she moves away. Her head low

like before with her sad eyes.

I climb into the bin.

I pull out the end of a fizzy drink and a sandwich.

I drink the drink and eat half the sandwich and then
put the rest on the ground for the white dog.

She takes it and eats it.
She is so beautiful.

* * *

There are new restaurants opening all over
Moscow.
The women have blonde hair always, and the men
wear suits and gold rings. These men are gangsters
and they kill people.

They killed the two people in my block.
One, two. Silence.
One, two, and God counts.

In the bins outside is all the food they
can't eat because they are already fat.
Well, the women aren't fat, but all the men are.
At the very end of the night I go
to the restaurants and climb into the bins and
the white dog follows me there.
So I give her the thrown-out raw meat.

She won't take food from my hands

and won't let me touch her.

I think maybe someone hurt her.

* * *

Soundscape. Bonfire. Bombzi. Men *and* women.
  – *The potatoes are ready.*
  – *No they're not.*
  – *Yes they are.*

I am standing near two Bombzi.

They are roasting potatoes in their fire.

I'm not sure how to get near them without

being seen.

Then a gang of children come.

They get in a circle all round a Bombzi.

Soundscape. Children jeer at Bombzi.
Children.
  – *Bombzi drunks. Bombzi drunks.*
  – *Grab his trousers.*
  – *Go on, grab them.*
  – Bombzi – *What are you doing? Get off me. Don't. Don't.*

They push him on to the ground. The other Bombzi

can't do anything as there are too many children.

They push him to the ground and then take his

trousers off.

Soundscape.
– Bombzi – *What are you doing? Get off me. Don't. Don't.*
– Children – *Get his belt.*
– Children – *I've got it.*

They take all his clothes so he is

naked in the cold.

His old grey body shivers.

Soundscape. Children laughing.
  – *Look at his little legs.*
  – Bombzi – *Leave me alone.*
  – *Look at his willy.*
  – Bombzi – *Leave me alone.*
Children laughing.

I go to the fire while they are doing this, grab

two potatoes and run. No one sees me except the

white dog.

When I look back the children have pushed the fire

over and taken the other potatoes and a Bombzi has

fallen into the fire.

No one helps her.

Soundscape. Woman falling into fire. Screaming.
  – Bombzi – *Help! Help!*
Children laughing.

Bully boy is there and he is laughing very much.

The white dog runs with me and I run with her.

We run all the way back to the factory.

I put half of one of the potatoes on the ground,

It's a little nearer.

And she comes, snaps it up.

She eats it.

Then I put a piece in my hand.

I make my hand flat for her to take the potato.

It is hard for her.

I tell her I will never hurt her.

I remember my stepfather and his lying.

And I tell her I am not lying, I will not

hurt you, you are safe with me.

Soundscape. **Ivan** *sings.*

And then she takes the potato from my hand.

I am so happy.

I am so happy.

And I give her a name.

Belka.

Belka, who took food from my hand.

* * *

But I am not allowed in the den ever.

I try.

But Belka always barks 'no'.

I am never allowed in the den.

I have my own place, on the other side, at the back of the factory.

It is a good place under a fence with wire.

I have plastic boxes and a thick bit of cardboard and two pieces of carpet. One is on the ground, one I sleep under. It is warmer now but I am still cold at night.

The food I give her she takes back to her den, where she gives it to her other dogs.

Belka's dogs – they are all part of her den.

I give them names: they are Vano, Strelka, Ruslan and Kugya.

We hunt together.

In the mornings I go and beg for money.

Then I go and buy food and give it to my dogs.

We like biscuits and crisps.

Belka is always nearby.

We do this every day.

And late at night I go to the restaurants' bins.

These are the most dangerous places.

No one likes children or dogs.

So late at night is best.

* * *

But now is later on in the morning when

people are on their way to work.

I go down to the corner of Tverskaya Street

and beg.

I put my hand out flat.

People are in a hurry so you are safe.

A man stops and talks to me.

He gives me two hundred roubles.

He asks who I am.

Soundscape. Man.
   – *What is your name?*

What is my name?

I don't answer.

Soundscape. Man.
   – *I know somewhere really nice we can go that has ice cream.*

He says there is a nice place we can go

for ice cream. 'What's your favourite?' he says.

Soundscape. Man.

   – I bet it's chocolate, or is it strawberry? Is it strawberry?
   Or lemon? They do a good lemon sorbet there. Do you like
   chocolate chip ice cream? They will have all your favourites.
   Don't you trust me?

   Don't you trust me?

Soundscape. Man.

   – Come on, don't be silly, little boy. Come on! I've paid you.
   Come on.
   (Man continues shouting at **Ivan** *through text below.)*
   – Come on! Come on, you
   stupid, stupid little boy. I've paid you. I've paid you!
   I tried to be nice but you wouldn't come.

   He starts shouting at me, then he grabs me.

   I don't know what to do. I know he is going to

   hurt me bad. I tell him to let go.

   But he won't let go of me.

   He starts dragging me away.

   He pulls me into a back street.

   I don't know what to do.

   So I bark.

Soundscape. **Ivan** *barks, with difficulty at first and then he*
howls – heartbreaking. It is the most extraordinary sound.
He repeats this howl.

   And then they are all there – Belka, Vano,

   Strelka, Ruslan and Kugya.

Soundscape. Man.
  – *Don't hurt me. There, there, doggy, doggy.*
  Dogs attack.

He lets me go.

We run all the way back to the den.

All the dogs are grinning now.

And.

And.

I touch her. I touch Belka.

She lets me feel her soft white fur.

And this, this is the first of the best days.

* * *

Vano is a silly dog and he always wants to play.

He is a big black dog with a large wet nose. He licks
me until I scratch his belly. Then he lies on me
and pants in my ear, and licks my face. And sometimes
Vano and I go out together on our own and we race
and hide until Belka barks and we must come home.

Once we chased squirrels in the park all afternoon.

And when we got home Belka growled and
snapped at us for being so naughty and staying
away too long.

Sometimes the dogs get cross with each other
and then Vano is very, very silly and makes us
laugh and rolls on the ground and runs off
with things.

Strelka and Ruslan run like the wind and
they are always guarding, like me. We
look out always. Strelka is strong and thin and
Ruslan is big and brown and his bark is
very cross always.

If they sleep when they are watching, Belka barks
at them.

So they are always a bit awake even when they
are sleeping. They hear everything.

Kugya likes to roll over in anything that smells.
He has thick brown fur and eyes that say yes
every day.

Belka tells us what to do.

We all stand still.

And listen.

To the wind, the cars, the

factory and the people.

No one likes us.

So we have to be very careful.

And then Belka nudges.

And we run again.

She knows when danger is near.

Belka knows best and we do whatever

she tells us.

I learn to growl. I learn to howl.

You howl when you can't find each other and

they howl back to say they are nearby. And then

when we are together we all growl at each other

but no one ever gets hurt. It's so we know if

we've been good or not.

Sometimes I fall asleep when I should be

watching out and then Belka wakes me up by

jumping on me and growling.

And every morning I unfold my mother's picture

and tell her how happy I am and that I hope
she likes dogs, but I know she does.
Because one day we will all be together.

* * *

It is so hot now that we never do anything in
the middle of the day.
They sleep in their den.
And I sleep in mine.

But Belka still won't let me into their den.
She barks 'no'
whenever I try.
I want to curl up with them, I want to be with them
all the time.
But she won't let me in.

I wake up for when the men go back
in from their lunch
so I can get what they have left in the bins.

There's a nice man, who is always clearing up.
He works in a restaurant near Tverskaya Street
and he gives me special bits that the fat gangster
men and their thin wives don't want.

He is not always there so I wait
and watch to see if he is working and when
he comes out for a smoke, I stand a little away,
with my head bent low, with sad, hungry eyes.

Then he goes back in and finds something for me,
and something for my dogs. Once it was a bar of
chocolate. I still shared it. I share everything with
my dogs.

We know every moment
what we need to see.
And where danger is.
And when to go.
We know now.

* * *

And now I am standing near the hole in the ground
that the children go down.
I am begging much further down the street than
where I go.
Today has been no good and no one has given
me any money to buy biscuits or drink with.
I think people have less again.

Some of the shops have nothing inside.

I think things are very bad.

It is dangerous to beg here as I know it belongs to

the other children. But I'm not worried.

And then there is shouting.

Soundscape. Boy.
   – *Hey you, what are you doing here?*

He's the bully boy, that made the children

have nothing in their eyes.

Soundscape. Boy.
   – *What are you doing here? This is my territory.*

But I am not scared.

Soundscape. Boy.
   – *Hey, you deaf or something?*

He comes closer.

Soundscape. Boy.
   – *I'm talking to you.*

Come close, I think. Come very close.

Soundscape. Boy.
   – *This is my territory. You listening?*

And then he runs towards me to push me.

But then I bark.

Soundscape. Dogs growling and snapping.

All my dogs are there.

They circle him.

They are very angry with him

for trying to hurt me.

And then he starts to cry.

He is crying and crying.

We go.

The bully boy doesn't move – he stays on the
ground in a small ball.

I think he is still crying.

* * *

I am waiting at the back of the restaurant.

The nice man has just gone in to get me and my
dogs something.

Then I turn and there is a militia man.

He grabs me hard and won't let go.

Soundscape. Man.
  – *Got you.*

But he is silly to do this.

I bark.

Soundscape. Dogs growling and barking.

> I say, 'They will bite you hard if you do not let me go.'

Soundscape. Man.
  – I'm not letting go.

> Vano leaps up at him.
>
> And now
>
> he lets me go.

Soundscape. Man shouting.
  – I'll get you. I'll get you. I'll be back, little git.

> We run and run.
>
> I can hear him shouting.
>
> If the militia capture you they put you in
>
> prisons filled with other children
>
> that no one cares about.

* * *

> It's a full moon. The summer is going.
>
> We go to the hills at the top of Moscow and look
>
> over the city, my dogs and me.
>
> And we howl.

From here the city glitters.

From here it doesn't smell.

There are no bins to spill rubbish and

no bully boys or drunk stinking Bombzi.

From here you can imagine a city of good.

From here God never has to count.

And somewhere in the city my mother is sleeping,

and he is not there any more, or maybe she is

dancing or out in a restaurant with somebody

nice, and I feel her curled-up picture in my pocket.

And Vano barks and Belka barks and we run round

and round and round. I am so happy.

* * *

So I go and see my mother.

Belka comes with me.

It is right across the city.

We start at the end of the night, when it is safer.

It is a long walk.

All the blocks look the same.

And then I see it.

I wait outside until someone goes in

and then slip in with them.

I climb up all the stairs and knock.

No one comes.

I knock again.

I wait.

Then a woman I don't know opens the door.

I don't know what to do.

I think she is drunk.

She tells me to go away and shuts the door.

Then Nina comes.

Soundscape. Woman.
Interior. Stairwell.

    – *Where have you been? Ivan, you look dreadful. They were so worried about you. Oh Ivan, you don't know, do you? You don't know.*

Then Nina stops talking.

And won't say anything.

I ask her where my mother is.

And she starts to cry.

And then,

and then she says that my mother is dead.

And everything goes silent.

'One.' Silent. 'One.' Silent.

'She died three months,' ago she says.

Soundscape. Woman.
  – *Ivan, I'm so sorry. So sorry. Come and have some hot milk.*
   Come in with me.

Nina tries to get me to come with her.

But I won't.

We go and wait outside, Belka and me.

We wait until it is dark.

We wait for him.

Soundscape. Stumbling man approaching. Mumbling to self. Man.
  – *Git. I'd have paid him tomorrow. Would have paid him.*

And now he is coming.

My stepfather.

Drunk like always.

I am bigger now.

It is easy.

I trip him up.

He falls.

Soundscape. **Ivan** *trips him up. Thud as he falls to the ground. Belka growls and corners him.*

Soundscape. Growling and snapping dog.
Man.
   – Get her off me. Get off me.
Ivan *kicks the 'imagined' man, Belka continues to bark and growl. Man groaning.*

And I kick him and kick him and kick him and kick
him and kick him and kick.

But he looks like an old man and

there is nothing in his eyes.

The vodka has eaten him up.

Belka barks – it's enough.

We leave him.

Lying curled up on the ground.

He doesn't even recognise me.

* * *

And it begins to rain a lot.

And the leaves in the park go brown.

Every day there is no sun and no stars.

Then Vano disappears.

One day he goes out and does not come back.

We wait for him.

When it is night and he should be home

Belka and the others howl for him

but he still doesn't come back.

They howl all night.

But still he doesn't come.

I go out looking for him.

The dogs won't come with me.

So I look on my own.

It is hard to be without them.

There is no kindness without them.

I see the bully boy walking towards me.

I turn to run.

Then I see he is not walking properly.

He looks much older.

He wobbles.

A Bombzi goes to him.

It is very cold.

So the Bombzi rubs vodka in his face,

to make his face warm.

And then he helps him stuff newspapers in his

shoes. This stops the cold.

They drink from a bottle.

He is a Bombzi too, I think now.

I think that is the only thing you can grow

up to be.

Vano still doesn't come back.

We are all quiet.

I try to go into the den.

Soundscape. Bark.

I try again.

Soundscape. Bark.

She still won't let me in.

Maybe Vano is lost somewhere.

Maybe he has been taken.

Maybe he is dead.

And maybe it was silent after he died.

When God is counting:

One, one, one.

One more for heaven.

I curl up into a little ball and cry.

I didn't cry for my mother.

But I cry for Vano.

I cry all night.

* * *

Now I am at the back of the restaurant again.

This time I am very careful.

I wait for the man but I always

have my dogs close by.

So I am always safe because they are here.

He goes inside to get me something.

I watch him, all the way. Ready to bark.

He has told me he likes children

and dogs.

Soundscape. Men.
   – *There he is.*
   – *Grab him.*
   – *I've got him.*

And then there is five militia.

They have big sticks.

But the dogs see.

Soundscape – dogs growling and barking.
Men.
   – *Hold him fast.*
   – *The dogs.*
   – *Hit them.*

But Vano is not here.

We are too little.

Soundscape. Russian Militia shouting as dogs attack. Yelping dog.
Men.
  – *Keep hold of him.*
  – *Hit them. Hit them.*

They get hold of my legs and my arms.

And I howl.

They take me into the van.

I think they will take me away.

Soundscape. Ferocious snarling. Growling and biting. Screams
from men.

Then Belka is in the van.

She is going mad.

She looks like a wolf. Her eyes are red

and her teeth bite into the men,

through their clothes and into their skin.

She will not let them take me.

She is so angry with them.

And they let me go.

She makes them let me go.

Soundscape. More shouting from Men.
  – *We'll get you next time, dog boy. And your dogs.*
  – *They've cut into my skin.*

And I am out of the van.

And we run like the wind.

We run and run and run.

And I slip but then I am back on my feet again.

Away from the den in case they follow

us and then back to it.

They don't know all the ways.

We know all the ways.

All the secret animal ways.

Belka knows I am very frightened.

There is a red mark on my neck where the militia

hit me.

On that night the first snow comes.

And it is very, very cold.

I don't know what to do.

If I stay out I think I might die.

I lie outside the dogs' den and bark.

Soundscape Belka barks back 'yes'.

It is a good bark.

I think she might let me in now.

I bark again.

She barks back another good bark.

I crawl inside.

It is dark and warm.

I lie curled up with their warm bodies

all around me.

I put my head in their soft fur.

I am buried in their warm fur, in our den,

and the cold can't creep in and hurt me.

I know Belka loves me and I love her too.

And nothing matters any more.

Any more.

Now I am dog.

* * *

And now

people don't give anything.

I think there is even less money for people now.

Even the kiosks have nothing.

The dogs and me are hungry all the time.

The men don't come out to eat their lunch

because it's too cold, so nothing is in the bins

outside.

But every night I am let into the dogs' den, our den.

And I curl up with Belka and the others.

And then nothing is bad with the world.

And all the world is happy, safe in her warm

white fur.

* * *

But now we are very, very hungry.

So I think I must go back to the restaurant.

I will be careful.

And my dogs will be with me.

So we go.

I wait for the man.

He comes out for a smoke.

He sees me and then goes back in.

He is a long time.

I can't see my dogs.

But I know they are near.

They were just behind the bins but now I can't see
them. But they must be near. They are always near.

I wait.

It is not good to wait so long.

I look for them again. I am about to bark, to be sure
they are there, when he comes back.

Soundscape. Man.
  – *It's for you.*

He has three chocolate bars
and some milk.

Soundscape. Man.
  – *I need to have the glass back.*

He says I have to drink it now and give him the
glass back otherwise he will get into trouble.

I go to him.

He tells me not to be afraid, that he won't
hurt me.

Soundscape. Man.
  – *There is nothing to be afraid of. Come on, we're friends, aren't we?*

I snatch the glass and chocolate off him and back
away and drink it.

But something is wrong.

I know something is wrong.

Then militia come. (*stop*)

Soundscape. Man.
  – *There he is.*

There are eight of them.

I bark.

No one comes.

Soundscape. Man.
  – *Got him.*

I bark again.

No one comes.

Soundscape. Men.
  – *You can bark all you like, dog boy.*
  – *No one's coming for you.*

Where are they?

I howl. I howl and howl.

Still they don't come.

Soundscape. Men.
  – *No one's coming for you.*
  – *We've seen to them.*
Men laugh.

Belka! Belka! Belka!

Then I scratch and bite.

What have they done to them?

Why don't they come?

I howl like there is nothing. Nothing any more.

Soundscape. Putting **Ivan** *into a van.*
   – Well done.
   – Easy. As easy as picking up a five-year-old, eh, boys?
Sound of real wolf repeatedly howling.
Men.
   – Get him to be quiet.
   – Shut the little shit up.

I howl and howl.

*Soundscape. The agonising howling of a real wolf continues,
followed by a thud and an abrupt silence.*

They hit me in the van and I stop.

They would have trapped them with food,

That's what they did.

They trapped them with food

because they were so hungry.

They told me in the van.

And then they said about my dogs,

about Belka, Strelka, Ruslan, Kugya.

Belka, Strelka, Ruslan and Kugya.

One, two, three, four.

One, two . . .

Ivan *tries to continue counting but cannot – imagining the 'three' and 'four' in his head.*

Four more for heaven.

Sshh.

Four more.

Sshh.

There you go.

Up to heaven with you.

Sshh.

* * *

I won't say about the orphanage.

Those were the worst days.

Worse than ever before.

There were bully boys and younger boys who wet
their beds and cried all night long.

And they take me to church.

And tell me I have a soul.

It is the thing that has to be counted out
when you die. 'One.' 'One.'

It is a shiny thing that sits inside me and is a bit of
God but when I look at it, at this bit of God,
it has a tail, and paws, and a black wet nose – and
it can hear the sound of a man's whisper from
three hundred metres, the fall of snow and the ice
breaking on the Moskva River from the other side
of the city.

It can hear jackdaws, and sparrows and
other wild things – the wild things that are around
us always – in the middle of the city. It is dog.

* * *

Then a woman starts to visit.

I tell her to go away.

I tell her that she's not a dog so what's the point
of her.

I tell her that all humans lie.

I tell her dogs don't lie.

I tell her that everything is made up by humans.

I tell her that humans have made the past and the
future up to make ourselves up, so

they are one big lie.

Dogs just are. They don't make up stories.

I tell her humans only do bad things. So go away.

And I tell her that the only reason she wants me
is because of my time with the dogs.

Journalists come and take photos of me.

I won't talk to them.

I won't be a lie like all humans.

I want my dogs.

I want my dogs back.

But she keeps coming.

And one day I hear her shouting and shouting
at a journalist about me and telling them to leave
me alone.

So then I let her take me home.

There are no bully boys here

and no one cries all night.

And she is called Erina.

Soundscape. Music box.
Singing beneath text.

And on that first night she gives me a music box

and hot milk and I lift the lid of the box and it

plays music. And then she sings to me.

Soundscape. Lullaby and music box.

The music box has red patterns on it.

And it belonged to her grandmother and it is

'a gift'.

And I decide to stay with her.

Soundscape. Lullaby ends.

She has a stupid dog.

He has to be kept on a lead and likes to play

fetch in the house.

I won't play with him.

He is an idiot.

He never barks or growls or anything.

Then one day when we are sleeping

someone breaks in.

And the dog goes mad, and we wake up with him
barking and growling, and he is biting and
hurting the man. And the bad man runs away.

And then I see her.

Soundscape. Lullaby intro. (No words.)

I look into the dog's wild eyes, and see her.
And I am grinning and then the dog is grinning.
I see Belka deep in his eyes.
Belka is there.

She is in all dogs everywhere.
Deep down at the bottom of their eyes.
She is everywhere.
And always.

And we go back to bed.
And I let the dog sleep on my bed.
And Erina sings.

Soundscape. Russian lullaby.

Bai, bai, bai, bai,
Báyu, Detusku mayú!
Bai, bai, bai, bai,
Báyu, Detusku mayú!
Shta na górki, na goryé,
O visyénnei, o poryé,

Ptíchki Bozhiye payút,
F tyómnam lyési gnyózda vyut.

> And I fall into a deep sleep.

Soundscape. Refrain of lullaby – into exterior of city and nocturnal animals – into forest at night.

> I see my dogs, all of my dogs.

> They are singing to me:

> Vano, Strelka, Ruslan, Kugya and Belka.

> We're down in the dark city and it's very

> cold. Belka goes still and we all stand and wait.

> Suddenly she barks and we run, and run into the

> wild, wild forest,

> into forever.

> Into now. And this is now.

> Running and running with my dogs in the white

> falling snow.

Ivan *exits. Soundscape. Lullaby. Imagery at back of space of a small boy sitting on the back of a wolf, among a pack, disappearing into a forest as snow falls.*

25619668R00039

Printed in Great Britain
by Amazon